kunar

Kunar

Paved Road
Dirt Track
District Border
River
Provincial Center
City

LOWER ELEVATION — HIGHER ELEVATION

Pakistan

Nuristan

Laghman

Nangarhar

Do Kalam
Bari Kot
Naray
Naray
Saw
Bargam
Nishigam
Ghaziabad
Asmar
Asmar
Dangam
Dangam
Sholtan
Shigal
Shigal
Marawara
Watapoor
Marawara
Asadabad
Asadabad
Sarkani
Sarkani
Nawa Pass
Watapoor
Narang
Narang
Pahshad
Nangalam
Manogai
Manogai
Chowkai
Khas Kunar
Loy Kalay
Chowkai
Khas Kunar
Chapadara
Spin Juna
Chapadara
Noorgal
Gol Salak
Noorgal

Table of Contents

Acronyms and Key Terms. vi

Guide to the Handbook. viii

Chapter 1: Overview and Orientation. 1

Orientation. 2

Relevant Historical Issues 7

Chapter 2: Ethnicity, Tribes, Languages and Religion 13

Ethnicity 13

Languages 15

Tribes 15

The Role of Religion 18

Chapter 3: Government and Leadership. 21

How the Government Officially Works 21

How it Actually Works 23

Security Forces. 24

2009 Elections 26

Political Parties. 27

Leader Profiles. 28

Chapter 4: The Economy 35

    Infrastructure 37

    Key Economic Sectors 38

    Trends and Relevant Issues for Kunar Today 40

Chapter 5: International Organizations and Reconstruction Activity . 43

    Provincial Reconstruction Team (PRT) 43

    National Solidarity Program 49

    Other International Actors and Projects 50

Chapter 6: Information and Influence 53

    Media Activity and Influence 53

    Information Sharing Networks 56

Chapter 7: Big Issues 59

    Economic Underdevelopment 59

    Nascent Security Forces 60

    Timber and Gemstones Smuggling 61

    Weak Governance 61

    Porous Border 63

Appendices 65

    Common Compliments 65

    Common Complaints 65

    Timeline of Key Events 66

    Day in the Life of a Rural Kunari 67

    Further Reading and Sources 68

List of Tables and Maps

LIST OF TABLES

Table 1. District Populations. 5

Table 2. Provincial Government 33

Table 3. International Organizations in Kunar. 51

LIST OF MAPS

Map 1. Population Density Map of Kunar. 4

Map 2. Major Tribes of Kunar. 14

Map 3. Economic Map of Kunar .36

Map 4. Conflict Map of Kunar. 54

Acronyms and Key Terms

ABP	Afghan Border Police
ACNP	Afghan Counter Narcotics Police
ADP/E	Alternative Development Program for the Eastern Zone
ADT	Agribusiness Development Team
AICC	Afghanistan International Chamber of Commerce
AISA	Afghanistan Investment Services Association
ANA	Afghan National Army
ANP	Afghan National Police
AWCC	Afghan Wireless Communication Company
BEFA	Basic Education for Afghanistan
BHC	Basic Health Center
CA	Civil Affairs
CDC	Community Development Council
CERP	Commander's Emergency Response Program
CHC	Comprehensive Health Center
CID	Criminal Investigation Division
COIN	Counterinsurgency
CSO	Central Statistics Office
DDS	District Development Shura
DIAG	Disbandment of Illegal Armed Groups
DoS	US Department of State
FATA	Federally Administered Tribal Areas
FOB	Forward Operating Base
GIRoA	Government of the Islamic Republic of Afghanistan
HIG or HIH	Hezb-e Islami Gulbuddin ("Islamic Party" formed by Gulbuddin Hekmatyar)
HIK	Hezb-e Islami Khalis ("Islamic Party" formed by Mohammad Yunus Khalis)
HP	Health Post
HTS	Human Terrain System

ICRC	International Committee of the Red Cross
IDLG	Independent Directorate for Local Governance
IED	Improvised Explosive Device
IMC	International Medical Corps
IO	International Organization
IRoA	Islamic Republic of Afghanistan
ISAF	International Security Assistance Force
ISI	Inter-Services Intelligence (Pakistan)
Jamiatis or JI	Jamiat-e Islami ("Islamic Union")
MADERA	Mission d'Aide Des Economies Rural Afghanistan
Meshrano Jirga	Elders' Assembly, upper house of Afghan National Assembly
MRRD	Ministry of Rural Rehabilitation and Development
MoE	Ministry of Education
MoI	Ministry of the Interior
MoPH	Ministry of Public Health
MoPW	Ministry of Public Works
Mustafiat	Department of Finance
NATO	North Atlantic Treaty Organization
NDS	National Directorate for Security
NGO	Non-Governmental Organization
NSP	National Solidarity Program
NWFP	North West Frontier Province
PC	Provincial Council
PDC	Provincial Development Council
PRT	Provincial Reconstruction Team
RAH	Reconstruction Agency of Hindu Kush
SCA	Swedish Committee for Afghanistan
UN	United Nations
UNAMA	United Nations Assistance Mission in Afghanistan
UNOPS	United Nations Office for Project Services
USACE	US Army Corp of Engineers
USAID	US Agency for International Development
USDA	US Department of Agriculture
USG	United States Government
VOA	Voice of America
Wali	Governor
Wolesi Jirga	People's Assembly, lower house of Afghan National Assembly
Woluswal	District Administrator

Guide to the Handbook

This handbook is a concise field guide to Kunar for internationals deploying to the province. Field personnel have used these guides in Afghanistan since June 2008 to accelerate their orientation process and to serve as a refresher on different aspects of the province during their tour.

Reading this book will provide a basic understanding of the people, places, history, culture, politics, economy, needs and ideas of Kunar. Building upon this understanding can help you:

- build rapport and a regular dialogue with local leaders,

- plan and implement pragmatic strategies (security, political, economic) to address sources of instability,

- influence communities to support the political process, not the insurgents, and

- build the capacity and legitimacy of a self-sufficient Afghan government and economy.

As you read the handbook and continue your inquiry in the province, seek to understand the influential leaders and groups in your local area and what beliefs and relationships drive their behavior. Think about the sources of violence in the area and whether groups are pursuing interests in a way that promotes conflict or stability. Finally, consider how various types of activities – key leader engagement, development assistance, security operations, security assistance, or public diplomacy – can effectively influence communities to work within the political process and oppose insurgency.

SOURCES AND METHODS

These handbooks are not intended as original academic research but as concise, readable summaries for practitioners in the field. The editorial team relies on their collective field experience and knowledge of the province as well as key sources such as the official Islamic Republic of Afghanistan (IRoA), United Nations and United States Government (USG) publications, and those sources listed in the appendix.

The editors made every effort to ensure accuracy. It should be noted, however, that there is often considerable disagreement regarding what is "ground truth" in Kunar, and things are constantly changing. As such, consider this book part of your orientation, and not an all-inclusive source for everything you need to know.

Information in this handbook is unclassified. The views and opinions expressed in this handbook are those of IDS International and in no way reflect the views of the United States Government or the United States Army.

THE ELECTRONIC UPDATE

Look for electronic updates to this book at *www.idsinternational.net/ afpakbooks*. Updates will cover any new developments, issues, and leaders that have emerged after publication. They will also provide corrections and expanded content in key areas based on feedback from readers.

We hope the handbook will continue to be a valuable tool in thinking about the challenges in Kunar. If you have questions, comments, or feedback for future updates or editions please email *afpakbooks@idsinternational.net*.

ABOUT IDS INTERNATIONAL

Publisher of Afghanistan Provincial Handbook Series and the FATA/NWFP Pakistan Books

This book is one of a series of handbooks on Afghanistan provinces and regions of Pakistan. Titles include Ghazni, Helmand, Kandahar, Khost, Kunar, Laghman, Nangarhar, Nuristan, Paktya, and Paktika. Pakistan titles include NWFP and FATA.

In addition to publishing these handbooks, IDS International provides training and analysis to government and private organizations in the areas of politics, economics, culture, stability operations, reconstruction, counterinsurgency, and interagency relations. In particular, IDS is a leading trainer of the US military in working with Provincial Reconstruction Teams (PRTs) in Iraq and Afghanistan. IDS offers its clients expertise and experience in the difficult work of interagency collaboration in complex operations. The writers and editors on this project offer a lifetime of experience working in these provinces and share a dedication to bringing peace and prosperity to the people of Afghanistan.

Author: Marina Kielpinski
Editors: Nick Dowling and Tom Praster
Assistant Editors: Tom Viehe and Chris Hall

IDS INTERNATIONAL GOVERNMENT SERVICES

1916 Wilson Boulevard

Suite 302

Arlington, VA 22201

703-875-2212

www.idsinternational.net

afpakbooks@idsinternational.net

PUBLISHED: JUNE 2009

This and other AfPak handbooks may be bought in either hard copy, digital, or audiobook format. Samples are available upon request. IDS International is also a leading provider of training and support on the cultural, political, economic, interagency, and information aspects of conflict. Direct all inquires to *afpakbooks@idsinternational.net* or call 703-875-2212.

Kunaris typically live in compounds of mud-brick homes. In the lowlands, these homes are single story, but in higher elevations, they can be two or three stories. Coniferous forests once blanketed the mountains of Kunar. However, decades of unchecked logging stripped the slopes down to rocky ridges, where Kunaris homes now rise up alone along the valley walls.

PHOTO BY MARINA KIELPINSKI

Chapter 1
Overview and Orientation

Kunar province is notable for its Pashtuns, its proximity to Pakistan, and its violence. It has played a strategic role in conflicts throughout both ancient and recent history. Today, Kunar sits at the crossroads between the lawless influence of the insurgency, mostly based across the border, and the developing legitimacy of the fledging provincial government. Even though Kunar is a small province, its strategic importance in the counterinsurgency has made it the frontline effort for military forces of the coalition and the Afghan national government north of the Tora Bora mountains.

Kunar is primarily mountainous, with its people living mostly along its river valleys. The Hindu Kush mountains dominate the landscape, rising to heights of 4,267 meters in the north. The Kunar River winds its way southwest from Pakistan's glacial slopes into Kunar, flowing across the full length of the province and continuing on to Nangarhar. In the south, the river slows and broadens at the widest part of the valley, nourishing the fertile fields of the southern districts. The mountains to the east are criss-crossed with paths to Pakistan. To the west of Asadabad, the narrow Pech River Valley produces gemstones, illegal timber, and a tenacious insurgency. Rugged mountains and thick forests isolate the notorious Korengal Valley from the rest of the province and provide a haven for insurgents. Over the centuries, the valleys have served as trade routes, sanctuary, and as the gateway to Jalalabad and eastern Afghanistan. The border with Pakistan is porous, mountainous, and challenging to control.

The vast majority of Kunar's population is Pashtun, though there are numerous sub-tribes with distinctive dialects and traditions. The nomadic Kuchi make Ghaziabad district in the north their primary summer grazing area, and Pashai communities populate the Mazar Valley. Nuristanis and Gujars live in the northern districts, and pockets of Tajiks can be found around Asadabad.

In years past, thick coniferous forests blanketed Kunar's mountains. But decades of unchecked logging stripped the hills down to rock and stubbly grass. The remaining strands of true forest are far from the main roads, on inaccessible mountain ridges or deep in roadless valleys. Shepherds graze sheep, and goats on steep hillsides dotted with small trees and shrubs. Asadabad, the capital of the province, has large irrigation canals, while smaller, hand-dug canals proliferate in the tributary valleys. Square compounds of mud-brick, single-story homes sprawl over the lowlands, and two- and three-story mud-brick homes rise up the valley walls in the steeper mountains. Farmers maximize scarce land by terracing the hillsides. Except for semi-precious gemstones and timber, Kunar produces little for trade or export, and its people continue to suffer from low literacy, lack of electricity, and limited access to health care and education.

ORIENTATION

Located in the northeast of Afghanistan, Kunar is bordered by the provinces of Nuristan to the north, Laghman to the west, and Nangarhar to the south. To the east, Kunar shares a 240-km border with Pakistan's North West Frontier Province (Chitral and Lower Dir districts) and the tribal agencies of Bajaur and Mohmand within the Federally Administered Tribal Areas (FATA). The province covers 3,742 square kilometers, or just over a million acres.

The two corridors of economic and political power are the Asmar Valley, running northeast to southwest from Naray in the north through Ghaziabad, Asmar, Shigal, and Dangam districts; and the Pech Valley, west of Asadabad, following the Pech River through Watapoor, Manogai, and Chapadara districts. The districts on the east bank have been isolated from the rest of Afghanistan, and are tied to Pakistan by geography, tribe, and family. The dynamics in eastern Kunar are shifting profoundly, however, with the construction of five vehicle bridges across the Kunar River, enabling easy access to trade and services in Asadabad.

Districts

Kunar has 15 districts including the capital, Asadabad (see Table 1). District boundaries are relatively new; people orient themselves by valleys, the key geographical feature of Kunar. The two major valleys, Asmar Valley and Pech Valley, follow the Kunar River and the Pech River, respectively, and pass through several districts. Most villages are nestled in narrow valleys, except in the flatter land in the south.

The northern districts of Naray and Ghaziabad border Nuristan and are home to mixed populations with many ethnic Nuristanis. The border is disputed; it was drawn in 2004 and some people do not agree with the boundaries. Some villages in this area prefer to be a part of Nuristan, while others want to belong to Kunar. The governors of Kunar and Nuristan held a shura in early 2009 to address this issue.

Following the Kunar River south toward Asadabad, the districts of Asmar, Dangam, and Shigal are smaller and have traditionally been power centers for commanders. In the south, the districts of Khas Kunar, Sarkani, and Chowkai have large populations and the most agricultural land. Noorgal, bordering Nangarhar province, is the most stable and peaceful district. Manogai district is the most volatile, home to the notorious Korengal Valley and the Shuriak Valley, where insurgents control the area and the government has no presence. Chapadara, in the far west, borders Nuristan and Laghman provinces and sees significant insurgent activity. Its land is covered in forest, which the people have decided to preserve by forbidding logging.

Pakistan

Nuristan

Laghman

Nangarhar

Do Kalam
Bari Kot
Naray
Naray
Saw
Barqam
Nishigam
Asmar
Dangam
Asmar
Dangam
Ghaziabad
Sholtan
Shigal
Shigal
Marawara
Watapoor
Marawara
Asadabad
Asadabad
Sarkani
Sarkani
Nawa Pass
Watapoor
Nangalam
Narang
Narang
Pahshad
Khas Kunar
Manogai
Manogai
Chowkai
Chowkai
Khas Kunar
Chapadara
Loy Kalay
Spin Juma
Chapadara
Noorgal
Noorgal
Gol Salak

Table 1. District Populations

DISTRICT	CENTER	TOTAL POPULATION	MAJOR TRIBAL GROUPS
Asadabad	Asadabad	29,177	Safi, Salarzai, mixed
Asmar	Asmar	20,716	Mushwani, Salarzai
Chapadara	Chapadara	28,681	Safi
Chowkai	Chowkai	28,905	Safi, Shomash
Dangam	Dangam	15,509	Mushwani, Salarzai
Ghaziabad	Ghaziabad	23,663	Nuristani, Mushwani, Gujar, Kohistani, Gorbati
Khas Kunar	Khas Kunar	31,950	Safi, Salarzai, Mohmand
Manogai	Nangalam	44,958	Safi, Salarzai, Korengali
Marawara	Marawara	17,316	Mamund, Salarzai
Narang	Narang	27,937	Safi
Naray	Naray	32,510	Kohistani, Gujar, Nuristani, Mushwani, Gorbati
Noorgal	Noorgal	25,047	Safi, Pashai
Sarkani	Sarkani	24,080	Mohmand, Mushwani
Shigal	Shigal	33,781	Mushwani, Gujar
Watapoor	Watapoor	28,778	Safi, Salarzai
Total		**413,008**	

Source: CSO/UNFPA Socio Economic & Demographic Profile, 2006
Tribal details from multiple interviews with local sources

Key Towns

Asadabad is Kunar's capital city and its only municipality. It is situated at the junction of the Kunar and Pech rivers and surrounded by rocky, treeless mountains and agricultural lands. Recent efforts by the municipality to clean up the streets have improved the city's appearance somewhat, but its grimy, rough collection of shops and houses are a testament to its poverty and troubled history. A traffic circle manned by Afghan police lends some control to the constant traffic of taxis, "jingle trucks," pedestrians, and donkeys. The dusty streets are lined with open ditches and wooden shacks where shopkeepers sell vegetables, fruits, spices, shoes, and fabric. The downtown area is dominated by a large mosque, a traffic circle, lumber yards, and a haphazard collection of two-story shopping centers. The newest buildings are a two-story school and the governor's office, built with funding from the US government. The road from Jalalabad is paved and in good condition; the trip takes about two hours by car.

The "second city" is **Chowkai,** a mainly Safi area south of Asadabad along the Kunar River and on the main road to Jalalabad. Chowkai sprawls over a flood-plain area and marks the mouth of the Dewagal Valley. Its location on the main road has spurred new growth, and it boasts a computer training center, a health clinic, and three-story shopping center. Green fields surround the town and lead up into the Dewagal Valley.

Nangalam in the Pech Valley (Manogai district) is the main bazaar town for several valleys: Shuriak, Korengal, Waygal, and Parun. The road connecting Nangalam to Asadabad follows the Pech River and was paved in 2007, facilitating access for the two key valleys that meet there – Chapadara and Waygal. Nangalam hosts the district center and the US military base Camp Blessing and has a busy downtown center with a new traffic circle and the Bahrain Hotel.

Minor towns include **Bari Kot** (border crossing with Pakistan), **Watapoor**, **Shigal**, and **Asmar**. The majority of people live in small villages.

RELEVANT HISTORICAL ISSUES

From Ancient to Modern Times

Permanent settlers have occupied Kunar's valleys for more than 2,200 years. Ruled by various strongmen and warring tribes, Kunar has strong traditions of Pashtun culture and strict adherence to Islam. No foreign army has managed to subdue Kunar. Alexander the Great was turned away in 330 BC, and the Indian empire, which eventually extended to Laghman, never included Kunar. Neither the British nor the Russians were able to subjugate the province during the "Great Game," and the British suffered major defeats at Chitral Arnawy and Chamarkand.

The Durand Line, the disputed border drawn in 1893 by British official Sir Mortimer Durand that bifurcated the Pashtun heartland, was imposed on Kunar nonetheless. The Afghan king who signed the treaty claimed that the border was invalid because he did so under duress. This point became moot in 1994, when many Afghans claim the 100-year-old treaty expired. The tribes that were divided by the Durand Line have never accepted it, and people continue to move back and forth on the many pathways and roads across the mountains.

Communist Era (1979-1992)

Kunar and Nuristan call themselves the "cradle of jihad," after their immediate and fierce uprising against the Soviet invasion of Afghanistan in 1979. Kunar was a natural supply route to other provinces of Afghanistan and was the first province to be ruled by the Afghan mujahedin. Communist forces used brutal methods to quell the resistance, almost totally destroying the town of Nangalam, where mujahedin leaders were based. In Kerala, just north of Asadabad, communist forces killed an estimated 1,200 men and boys in what became known as the Kerala Massacre. Many were wounded and buried alive along with the dead in a mass grave that is still visible along the river. Many members of Kunar's current leadership earned credibility with the people by fighting the Soviets, including General Jalal, now chief of police; Haji Rozi, head of the Program Takhim-e Sohl (PTS); and Haji Zalmai, district governor of Watapoor.

Mujahedin and Taliban (1989-2001)

The departure of the Soviets left mujahedin leaders to vicious infighting and competition for resources and power. Timber and gemstone smuggling financed the ongoing conflict, and foreigners supported their chosen factions. Commanders secured power and sett up mini-empires that still influence Kunar's politics. The conservative Salafi sect led by Maulavi Jamil al-Rahman gained prominence and brought Wahabbism to the fore. Thousands of civilians fled to Pakistan, staying in refugee camps or with relatives from across the border. The Taliban arrived in the chaos, promising to restore order. Top mujahedin commanders switched sides and secured resources for their militias. The Taliban soon fully controlled Asadabad, occupying the government offices and extending their authority into some of the districts. But the population quickly grew disenchanted with the Taliban's oppressive regime and lack of economic development.

Contemporary Events

One night in October 2001, a single US bomb hit a Taliban weapons depot in downtown Asadabad. By the next day the Taliban were gone, exiting via Ghakhi Pass into Pakistan. Mujahedin commanders swept into Asadabad and reclaimed control of the government offices, dividing power among themselves. Haji Jan Dod became the first governor, Matiullah Khan became the chief of police, and Malik Zarin commanded the border police.

From mid-2002 onward, Kunar's leadership cooperated with the central government in Kabul. Yusuf Shah Juhan, an outsider from Laghman province, was appointed governor in April 2002. The more radical elements, including Hezb-e Islami Gulbuddin (HIG) and the Salafists, steadily lost political influence.

Special Forces operated throughout the province with a light footprint, hunting al-Qaeda operatives and Taliban supporters. In late June 2005, a helicopter carrying US troops on a rescue operation to retrieve downed Special Forces was shot down in the Shuriak Valley, killing all 16 on board in the worst disaster in US Navy SEAL history.

The US PRT was set up at Camp Wright near Asadabad in 2004. The first battalion-size element from the 10th Mountain Division was set up at Camp Blessing in Manogai district in 2006. The introduction of US forces to the Korengal Valley stirred up resentment among locals and they once again took up arms to repel the outsiders. In 2009, an additional battalion of US troops reinforced ANA and ABP positions along the border.

The US PRT has steadily expanded its influence on the province's development and political landscape. Since 2008, key projects like roads and bridges are altering the way people live. The PRT and Governor Wahidi continue to have a close relationship. The effect of major infrastructure projects is beginning to be felt, though much work remains. The focus on roads has opened up access to previously isolated population centers. Small business growth is evident both in downtown Asadabad and in more remote areas. However, municipal governance structures are largely inadequate to capture greater and transparent revenue streams for funding public services.

In addition to the continuation of the road network, progress has been made to connect the previously isolated eastern section of the province to the government and people of Kunar proper. Five major bridges crossing the Kunar River are nearing completion. They will allow security forces better access to the previously isolated Pakistani side of the river, while enabling citizens to reach the public services and markets in Asadabad.

Despite progress in development and governance, Kunar remains a hotbed of violence. Increasing ANSF and ISAF presence disrupts insurgent transit routes and activities, and events in Pakistan's NWFP and FATA directly affect Kunar.

Many of the powerful figures who played key roles in Kunar's recent history – smugglers, commanders, and tribal leaders – continue to wield influence, and Kunar's leaders are struggling to find the balance between tradition and modernization. Modern governance is slowly making its impression on Kunar, but legitimacy depends on the government's ability to deliver justice, security, and basic services to the people. Kunaris are deeply suspicious and insular, sticking close to family and tribe. They have long lived according to their own customs and power structures, only loosely connected to higher government. This tradition of tribal governance was disrupted by the revolution and subsequent infighting; communities were divided, elders weakened, and time-tested methods of conflict resolution broken in the chaos. Families who traditionally ruled according to Pashtun customs were displaced by new rivals who gained power by amassing wealth and weapons rather than by earning legitimacy within the tribe. Now, as Kunar struggles to rebuild, these leaders (who are still not seen as legitimate by their communities) claim to represent the people. New power structures built on illegal industries, such as gemstones and timber, are imposed on fractured traditional systems, creating further rifts.

Weekly tribal shuras often meet with US troops to discuss their concerns. Shuras are one of the two primary institutions by which tribes make decisions.

PHOTO BY SPC. GREGORY ARGENTIERI

Chapter 2
Ethnicity, Tribes,
Languages and Religion

ETHNICITY

Kunar has a mix of ethnic, tribal, and linguistic groups, the result of centuries of migration based on land and conflict. The vast majority are Pashtun, from various tribes who settled in their respective valleys over hundreds of years. The major minority group present is Nuristani, which also has many sub-groups. The population varies significantly from north to south, with large numbers of ethnic Nuristanis in the northern and western districts, and Pashtun Safi tribes controlling most of the southern districts and the Pech Valley. Small numbers of Tajiks, who have been largely assimilated into Pashtun society, live along the Pech Valley.

Gawar and Gujar people are separate ethnicities with their own languages and customs and live in Naray district. The Pashai are in Mazar Valley in Noorgal district and have their own language.

Kunar also has a population of nomads (Kuchis) whose numbers vary in different seasons. GIRoA estimates that 20 Kuchi communities move to Kunar each winter. The most important summer area for the short-range migratory Kuchi in Afghanistan is in Ghaziabad district of Kunar.

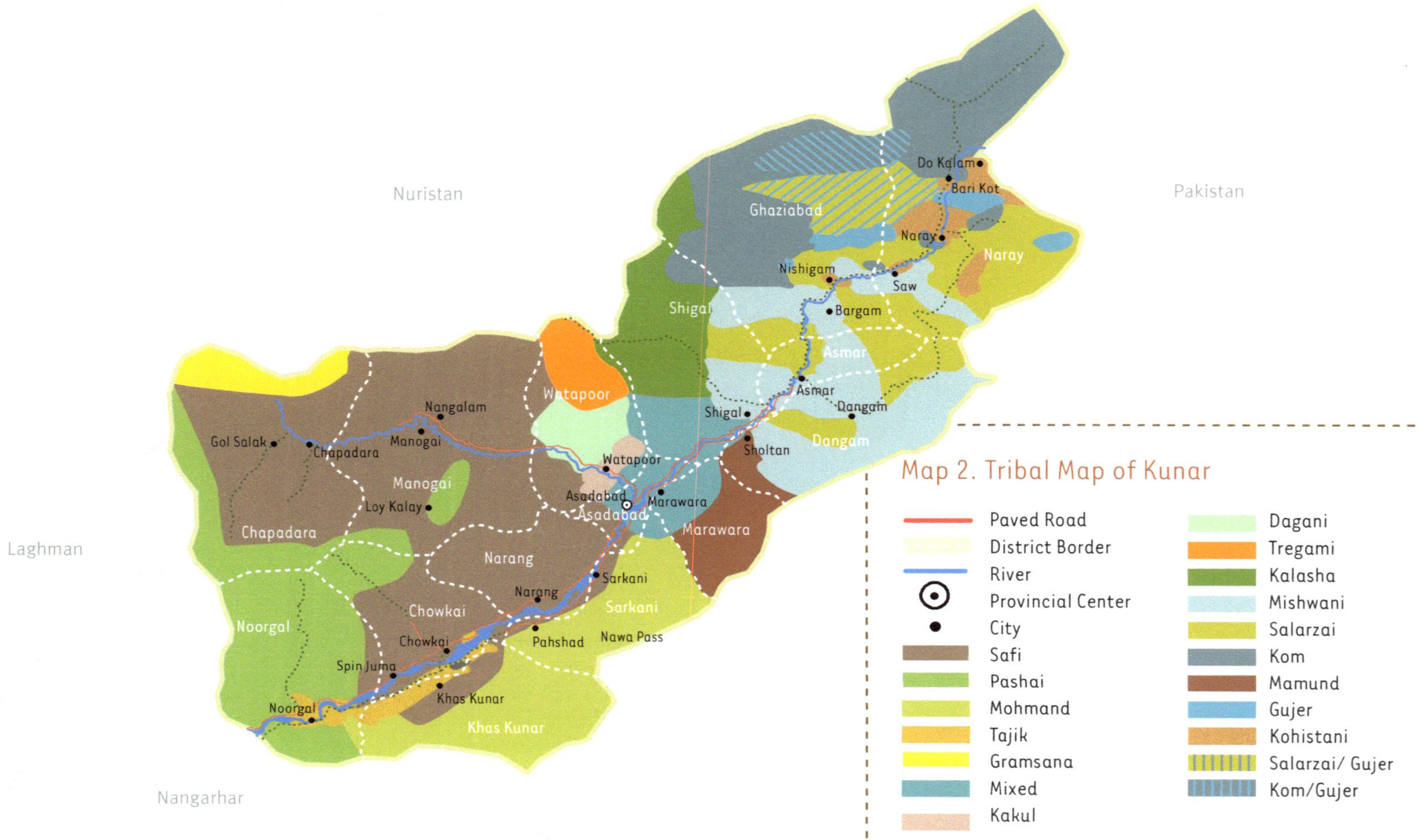

Map 2. Tribal Map of Kunar

Legend:
- Paved Road
- District Border
- River
- Provincial Center
- City

Tribes:
- Safi
- Pashai
- Mohmand
- Tajik
- Gramsana
- Mixed
- Kakul
- Dagani
- Tregami
- Kalasha
- Mishwani
- Salarzai
- Kom
- Mamund
- Gujer
- Kohistani
- Salarzai/ Gujer
- Kom/Gujer

Labels on map:
Pakistan, Nuristan, Laghman, Nangarhar

Places: Do Kalam, Bari Kot, Naray, Saw, Bargam, Nishigam, Asmar, Dangam, Dangam, Asmar, Sholtan, Ghaziabad, Shigal, Shigal, Marawara, Marawara, Watapoor, Watapoor, Asadabad, Asadabad, Sarkani, Sarkani, Nawa Pass, Nangalam, Manogai, Manogai, Loy Kalay, Narang, Narang, Pahshad, Chowkai, Chowkai, Khas Kunar, Khas Kunar, Chapadara, Chapadara, Spin Juma, Noorgal, Noorgal, Gol Salak, Noorgal

Kunar has a significant refugee returnee population. Thousands fled to Pakistan when the Soviets invaded and lost their land and homes. They returned in hopes of government assistance, and many now live in camps in Khas Kunar, waiting for assistance from the Department of Refugees and Returnees or UNHCR. However, the local population does not welcome the camps, and there is a shortage of land. Unemployed youth are easy recruiting targets for insurgents.

LANGUAGES

Nearly all people living in Kunar speak Pashto. Kunar's patchwork of languages and ethnicities deserves further study, and the concept of strictly defining groups and languages is a bit murky for most Kunaris. Nuristani, Gawar-Bati, and Gujar are distinct languages. Nuristani has several different dialects, none of which has a written form. Dari is mostly limited to educated people and government officials.

Translators generally speak at least three languages (Pashto, Dari, and English) and sometimes speak another dialect as well.

TRIBES

The tribe is the most powerful structure of Pashtun society, providing identity, security, and cohesion. Decades of conflict have weakened the tribes in Kunar but hardly threaten the existence of a centuries-old system. The modern government offers some services to the people, but it is limited in reach and still very weak. Tribal affiliation is still the key to loyalties and identity for Kunaris.

Tribal society prioritizes group harmony, using a group decision-making structure and relying on tribal elders for leadership. The goal of justice is to promote group harmony rather than punish an individual.

The two primary institutions are the *jirga* and the *shura*. A jirga is a tribal gathering convened specifically to solve a problem or reach a decision, and any decision made in a jirga is considered binding. A shura (from the Arabic word for consultation) is a more permanent council of elders who are responsible for security, justice, and local administration. Shuras have become more militarized in Afghanistan after decades of war, acting as short-term advisory councils that can include elders, commanders, and landowners. Shuras are a well-established tradition, and the National Solidarity Program (NSP) has formalized the structure to manage development needs at the local and district levels.

Prominent Tribes of Kunar

The **Safi** tribe dominates Kunar, and is divided into three sub-tribes: **Gurbuz**, **Musawud**, and **Wader**. They collectively control the Pech Valley and most major population centers.

The **Salarzai** are the second largest tribe in Kunar, but are scattered throughout the province. They live mostly in Shigal, but have sizeable settlements in Khas Kunar and Watapoor.

The third largest tribe, the **Mushwani,** are found mostly in Dangam, Shigal, Naray, and Ghaziabad. They are herders who migrated into the area 100 years ago.

The **Mamund** are heavily concentrated in Marawara, and a large number live across the border in Bajaur, Pakistan. They can be divided into "Big Mamund" and "Small Mamund" sub-tribes.

The **Shinwari** are mostly centered in Shigal district.

The **Mohmand,** distinct from the Mamund tribe of a similar name, mostly live in Khas Kunar and Sarkani.

The **Kohistani (also called Gawar)** are a mountain-dwelling people. They have distinct customs and their own dialect. They live in Naray and Ghaziabad.

Other Ethnic Groups

The **Gujar** are semi-nomadic and speak their own dialect (Gujar). Afghan Gujars are concentrated in Naray, Ghaziabad, Shigal, and Sarkani. Gujars are also found in large numbers in India and Pakistan.

The **Nuristani** have several sub-groups of people. All speak their own dialects, none of which are written.

The **Shomash** and **Pashai** mostly live in the Mazar Valley (Noorgal district). Larger numbers of Pashai live in the neighboring district of Dari Nur in Nangarhar. The people of the Korengal Valley are classified as Pashai as well and speak their own unique dialect of the Pashai language.

The **Kuchi** are nomadic herders who migrate throughout the country. Ghaziabad is their most important summer pasturing area, and they can be seen in Khas Kunar and Sarkani in the winter.

Drawing boundaries around tribes should be done with caution; they overlap one another and there are pockets of families scattered throughout the province. The map here is intended as a general guide.

THE ROLE OF RELIGION

Islam is the basis of life for Afghans in Kunar. Even if a person is not truly pious he will at least appear to be, and it would be unwise to challenge that. No outsider should ever speak poorly of Islam or accuse an Afghan of being un-Islamic. Outsiders can compliment someone for being a good Muslim, but the topic of religion should be approached lightly, if at all. Since Afghanistan is an Islamic Republic, there is no separation between religion and government. Any law made must be in line with Islamic principles.

Rural people rely on mullahs for religious interpretation, news from the outside world, and guidance. Mullahs are not traditionally powerful, but play an important role in legitimizing leaders. A fundamental problem is that many mullahs are hardly literate themselves. Poor families send their sons to Pakistan for education because a boy can receive free room and board in a Pakistani madrassa. Kunar has few madrassas and cannot provide such facilities to students. Some madrassas are supported by unknown donors and do not follow an officially condoned curriculum. Kunar's leaders talk openly of the need for official madrassas in Kunar.

Maulavi Naqibullah, the mullah of Kunar's largest mosque, is very cooperative with US forces and insists that he is defending Kunar from extremist ideology. The Directorate of Haj and Pilgrimage is the official government representative for the mullah community and religious matters, but people complain that the office is corrupt and ineffective.

Relevant Cultural Points: Beliefs, Prejudices, Behavior

Kunar is insular and conservative, strictly religious, and structured around *pashtunwali*, the code of ethics for the Pashtun tribe. Pashtunwali means "the way of the Pashtuns," and is a pre-Islamic code of conduct followed by the Pashtun tribes. All Pashtuns have knowledge of the code and follow it to some degree. Some tribes are stricter about the code than others.

Individualism is not a cultural value; group harmony is much more important. Pashtuns live in a highly structured society, and Kunaris strive for success as long as it is within the bounds of the accepted tribal ways.

Kunar's women are extremely constrained. Outside of a few members of the Provincial Council, the director of women's affairs, and a few doctors and teachers, women do not play a role in public life at all. Any outreach to women should be carefully coordinated through the appropriate channels – direct attempts to work with them will not be appreciated.

Appointed by President Karzai in 2007, Governor Sayed Wahidi has used his influence and political savvy to move many line directors and district sub-governors in a campaign against corruption. Describing himself as a social worker, Governor Wahidi is reaching out to tribal elders and mullahs in an attempt to incorporate traditional leaders into the official government.

PHOTO BY LT JAMES DIETLE

Chapter 3
Government and Leadership

Kunar's people are accustomed to government as a corrupt, incompetent, and predatory force. Traditionally, people rely on the tribal system to provide justice and local administration. However, the current provincial government has gained some credibility by delivering limited services, reaching out to tribal leaders, and making an attempt to curb corruption. Unlike his predecessors, Governor Wahidi regularly visits the districts and has made improvements in district governance. There is still widespread dissatisfaction. People blame the government for security problems and lack of economic development, but the mechanisms set up to coordinate assistance are building trust and helping to create the foundation for a more secure future.

HOW THE GOVERNMENT OFFICIALLY WORKS

Central Control

Authority and power in Afghanistan are concentrated in the national government as a means to counter the power of warlords in the provinces. As such, the provincial government is limited to an advisory role for the central government, while decisions on everything from policy to funding priorities are made in Kabul.

Provincial Government

A governor (*wali*) heads the provincial government and reports to the Independent Directorate for Local Governance (IDLG), located in the Executive Office of the president. A deputy and several staff that oversee provincial government management assist him.

Ministries in Kabul execute their policies and programs through departments located at the provincial level. Ministers, with the approval of the president, appoint provincial directors who manage the departments. The director reports to and receives funds from the ministry in Kabul. The governor does not have budgetary authority over any of these departments, but must approve all expenditures before they are processed by the Department of Finance (*Mustafiat*).

The Provincial Council (PC), an elected body at the provincial level, provides a voice for the people in advising on provincial issues. The PC reports directly to the president and has no budget. Its relevance largely depends on the governor's support and on its members' individual resources and ambition .

The Provincial Development Committee (PDC), including the governor and six department heads, is responsible for implementing the Provincial Development Plan (PDP) and coordinating with key players on development needs. External players such as the UN, PRT, and interested NGOs also attend meetings.

District and Local Governance

Government at the district level mirrors the provincial government with the *woluswal* (district governor or sub-governor), police chief, National Directorate of Security officer, clerks, and a small police force. Ministry sub-departments also operate at the district level, but are not present in every district. In 2007, District Development Assemblies (DDAs) were formed in order to plan, prioritize, and coordinate development activities at the district level. Below the district level, the only formal governance structures are the Community Development Councils (CDCs). These CDCs help MRRD manage the National Solidarity Program.

The municipality of Asadabad is led by a mayor, who is appointed by the IDLG in consultation with the governor. Municipalities are independent from the provincial government, are free to plan, fund, and implement projects, and can tax local businesses.

HOW IT ACTUALLY WORKS

Traditional mechanisms of authority and dispute resolution coexist uneasily with the formal provincial and district government. Powerful individuals (*maulavis*, *maliks*, and tribal elders) control their areas of influence. The justice sector is particularly weak; local courts often cannot act without endorsement of tribal elders. In parts of Kunar, a traveling Taliban judge hears cases and administers justice based on *sharia* law. There is a deep and abiding distrust of the national government (and its local manifestations) because of its competing claim to individual allegiance and the long historical experience of government as a predatory and disruptive force. In Kunar, there is some fear that the extension of authority of district officials (district governors) is undercutting traditional authorities and contributing to instability.

At a practical level, the provincial government works somewhat differently from the constitutional structure. Several of the departments operate independently; reform at the ministerial level means that some departments were folded into others, but they continue to maintain their own offices, staff, and activities in the provinces. Patronage networks are deeply rooted. Personalities play a determining role, and conflicts between directors can disrupt governance. Governor Wahidi is a modernist and has introduced greater transparency, but the lack of capacity in Asadabad and the districts hampers his efforts.

Departments receive limited support from their ministries in Kabul and are unable to respond to the needs of the people. Brain drain is also a problem; talented people often seek better jobs in Kabul or Jalalabad, or stay in Kunar to work for NGOs or US forces.

Governor Wahidi has used his influence and political savvy to shift many of the heads of departments and district governors around and continues to pledge a campaign against corruption. Several programs focus on improving governance, such as the Afghan government-led Public Administration Reform (PAR), USAID/DAI's Local Governance Capacity Development Program (LGCD), and the long-term Independent Administrative Reform and Civil Service Commission (IARCSC).

Tribal Tensions and Leadership

Governor Wahidi and his district governors are reaching out to elders and mullahs. Some traditional leaders are being incorporated into the official government, but others are resisting these overtures. District governors are the front-line coordinating body between the traditional tribal structures and the institutions of provincial governance.

SECURITY FORCES

Afghan National Police (ANP)

Kunar's police force, led by Brigadier General Jalal Jalal, is plagued by corruption, poor discipline, and institutional problems. US forces are training and equipping the ANP, but progress is slow. The distribution of forces (*tashkil*) is set in Kabul, and therefore reform at higher levels is required to get the appropriate coverage in Kunar. Enforcement is a problem since many police work in their home areas and do not command enough respect from the people. The ANP also has a competent counter-narcotics team, led by Colonel Sayed Rahim, which concentrates on poppy eradication and interdiction. The four top crimes the ANP deals with involve poppy, pedophilia, timber smuggling, and prostitution. DynCorps trainers work closely with the ANP to improve finance, personnel, training, logistics, and operations capabilities.

Afghan National Army (ANA)

The ANA has a good reputation in Kunar. People perceive the army to be a professional force with the ability to protect them from insurgents. Recruitment is not a problem, but there are still not enough soldiers. Their credibility will likely increase as they begin to conduct more independent operations. There are new ANA bases along the border with Pakistan, and units work closely with US forces to block insurgent transit routes.

National Directorate for Security (NDS)

The NDS is generally viewed as a professional, competent force. Jamiullah, the director, is a Nuristani who was educated in Kabul under the communist regime. The NDS has solid intelligence and operational capabilities. The NDS has staff in every district and is well equipped. Little is publicly known about the daily operations of the NDS.

Afghan Border Police (ABP)

The ABP is very weak in training, logistics, equipment, and discipline. It was shifted from the Ministry of Defense to the Ministry of the Interior in 2008 and suffers from a lack of government attention. However, US forces are providing training and equipment to the ABP, and a new headquarters compound was opened in Sarkani district in summer 2008 (funded by CSTC-A).

Security Coordination

Commanders from these security forces (ANP, ANA, and NDS) meet weekly with the governor, PRT, and other US forces to discuss security issues in the province. The Provincial Coordination Center (PCC), a joint US and ANSF 24-hour facility in the governor's compound, facilitates real-time information sharing.

2009 ELECTIONS

Presidential and Provincial Council elections are scheduled to take place on 20 August 2009. When President Karzai's term expired in May, he began serving as a caretaker president until elections could be held. Candidates for president filed in May, but few national contenders emerged, as President Karzai persuaded many of his rivals not to challenge him. In terms of security, Afghan National Security Forces (ANSF) will be extensively involved in the elections, recruiting 23,000 police and soldiers for the event. The security of the elections represents a potential key moment for the summer fighting season between Taliban and ANSF/ISAF. After the elections, changes in the Afghan government will include new senior appointments, including new ministers and governors. Late 2009 and 2010 will be a key period for these new officials to leverage their public mandate and expanded international assistance to deliver more accountable and credible governance to the Afghan people.

Kunar was among the first provinces to complete voter registration for the elections, and it went surprisingly well. The province even registered a record number of women. Observers anticipate security problems in districts like Ghaziabad and Chapadara, where insurgent activity has been on the rise. A basic challenge will be logistics – some of the more remote valleys like the Shuriak are difficult to access, and voters may have to travel to distant polling stations to cast their ballots. However, Kunar's citizens always show enthusiasm for elections. Though there will undoubtedly be security and logistical challenges, locals and international observers predict successful elections in Kunar.

A more detailed update on elections is included in the back folder of your book or can be downloaded at *www.idsinternational.net/afpakbooks*. The pre-election update goes into the elections process in greater detail and the post-election update will summarize the results and implications.

POLITICAL PARTIES

Kunar has many political parties, and loyalties are primarily based on tribe and wartime affiliations. Major political parties in Kunar are listed below in order of influence.

Hezb-e Islami Gulbuddin (HIG): A mujahedin militant group active since the Soviet invasion and led by Hekmatyar Gulbuddin. Actively opposed to US-led and Afghan national forces. The political arm of HIG is the most popular party in Kunar.

Hezb-e Islami Khalis (HIK): Originally a mujahedin group that broke away from HIG under the leadership of Yunus Khalis. It is led by Haji Din Mohammad, former governor of Nangarhar. An estimated 10 percent of Kunaris support this party, based on interviews with local leaders.

Hezb-e Afghan Millat (Afghan Nation Party): National Pashtun party, led by Finance Minister Dr. Anwar Ul-haq Ahadi. Widely popular in Nangarhar, this party has gained support in Kunar as well, particularly from the educated classes. Its platform is based on unity, security, and creating an Islamic version of democracy. Maintains a muted, ethno-nationalist rhetoric.

Ittehad-e Islami (Sayyaf): Wahhabi group that rose to prominence during the mujahedin era with funding from Saudi Arabia and Kuwait. Its influence is waning.

Jamiat-e Islami (Islamic Society): The party of former President Burhanuddin Rabbani and the oldest Islamic political party in Afghanistan. Rabbani's new party, United National Front, has no support in Kunar.

LEADER PROFILES

Key leaders in Kunar include those occupying official positions, insurgent leaders, religious figures, politicians, and criminals. Most are some combination of these. Below is a brief overview of the most important and powerful figures.

Government/Political Leaders

Sayed al Haj Fazlullah Wahidi, Governor: Governor Wahidi assumed office in November 2007. He describes himself as a social worker, not a politician. Born and raised in Nangarhar province, he is an ethnic Pashtun. He studied education at Kabul University, then worked in government briefly under Daoud as a clerk in the Ministry of Agriculture, but spent most of his professional life in the NGO community in Peshawar and Afghanistan. He chaired the Afghan NGO coordination body and is currently on the board of directors of International Council of Volunteer Agencies. Wahidi is well traveled, speaks fluent English, and works very closely with the PRT. He traveled to the US on a government exchange program in April 2008.

Brigadier General Abdul Jalal Jalal, Chief of Police: General Jalal comes from Badakhshan province, where he aligned with Jamiat-e Islami and fought with the mujahedin. He is from the same home district as

Burhanuddin Rabbani. An ethnic Tajik, he rose through the professional ranks of the ANP and was appointed chief of police for Kunar in 2006. He maintains close relations with Jon Dod and Malik Zarin. He is cooperative with US forces.

Jamiullah, Head of NDS: Educated in Kabul under the communist regime, Jamiullah is from Nuristan province and is generally well regarded in Kunar. He is cooperative with the governor and US forces, and maintains a network of effective agents in the districts.

Maulavi Ezatullah, Chairman of the PC: Recently replaced Haji Abdul Wali Khan as head of the PC (Haji Abdul Wali Khan remains as a member). He is young, from Watapoor district. He has played a constructive role in security shuras, notably in Chapadara.

Haji Abdul Wali Khan, Member of the PC: Matiullah Khan's cousin, and a leader of the Safi tribe. He gained wealth through the timber trade. He maintains his business activities and is aloof to US military.

Fazl Akbar, Executive Director for Kunar Province: A political survivor, Fazl Akbar has occupied this position through successive governors. He is the brother of Haji Rozi (director of the Program Takhim-e Sohl) and a former teacher. He comes from Manogai district and is a member of the Safi tribe. Akbar is rich and is involved in the timber trade. His family is also rich and many of his relatives have construction contracts with the PRT. His family supports the party of Mujaddidi. Akbar went to Pakistan during the Soviet invasion. Today, he is very cooperative with the PRT.

Meshrano Jirga (Elders' Assembly)

Roshan Alokozai: From Sarkani district, Pashad village, he supported the Khalq party during the jihad, along with Malik Zarin. He is neither popular nor well-known in Kunar now. He was appointed by President Karzai.

Haji Ghulam Sakhi, Senator: A member of Mushwani tribe, from Asmar, Sakhi is the cousin of Malik Zarin, with whom he has a long-standing feud. In 200,5 Malik Zarin accused him of having a weapons cache, so US forces raided his house and burned the compound. He approached the PRT commander and then-Governor Wafa many times for compensation and eventually received it. He is heavily involved in timber and owns a lumberyard in Kerala (northern Asadabad). He has a strong power base in Asmar and was easily elected to Parliament. He supported HIK but later worked with the Taliban.

Haji Saleh Mohammad: He is from Manogai district, Bar Kandai village. He was a small businessman with a shop selling spare parts for vehicles and ran for the Provincial Council. After gaining a seat there he moved on to the Meshrano Jirga. He is not very popular.

Wolesi Jirga (People's Assembly)

Maulavi Shahzada Shahid: An active HIG member from Chowkai district, Shahid is the former chief justice for Kunar and chief of the council of mullahs. He is educated, literate, and charismatic and continues to be popular.

Shija al Mulik Jalala: An HIG member from Ghaziabad district, he is perceived as honestly trying to do something to help people. He is helped by a brother in the US, supports health care and schools, and built a library in Ghaziabad. Jalala gained fame as the national chair of the district shura. He is married and has no children.

Gul Haar Jalal: He is widow of a Maoist from Naray district (Maoists are present in Naray district but relatively low-profile).

No member of parliament has a university degree or a proven track record of delivering assistance to the people. Some MPs have a solid support base but none is widely popular, except Maulavi Shahzada Shahid.

Tribal/Ethnic Leaders

Tribal and ethnic leaders hold sway among their own people, but there is no province-wide figure who derives his power from tribal or ethnic status. Some well-known leaders of the larger tribes are:

- Sub-Governor Haji Zalmai, Safi tribe (Watapor district)
- Malik Zarin and Haji Sakhi, Mushwani tribe (Asmar district)
- Fazl Akbar and Haji Rozi, Safi tribe (Manogai district)
- Mir Azam Gujarwal, Gujar tribe (Naray district)

Business Leaders

Malik Zarin: The most powerful figure in the Asmar area, Zarin is from Asmar district center, Mushwani tribe. He controls timber and some gemstone smuggling. Zarin has a longstanding blood feud with his cousin Haji Sakhi because he was the key jihadi commander fighting the Taliban when Haji Sakhi was working in the Taliban government. First to claim control of Kunar when the Taliban departed, many of his relatives, bodyguards, and associates were hired as security guards when the PRT was set up in Asadabad, and many of them still work for the PRT. Focused on business rather than religion, Malik Zarin has always allied with more liberal leaders such as Zahir Shah, Mujaddidi, and Karzai. Many believe he is supported by ISI. Malik Zarin is close to Karzai and was involved in the negotiations for the release of the kidnapped Italian journalist Daniele Mastrogiacomo in 2007.

Matiullah Khan: Khan is the most powerful figure in the Pech Valley. From Gulsalak village, Chapadara district and the Safi tribe, he controls timber and gemstone smuggling in that area. He became leader of Mahaz-e Milli party; later, he was commander of Pech Valley forces for the Taliban (against Jon Dod and Malik Zarin). He then allied with Malik

Zarin and Jon Dod to reclaim Asadabad when the Taliban departed and became chief of police in Kunar. He set up a construction company and won the PRT Nuristan contract to build a bridge in Kamdesh. He is now chief of police in Kapisa province and retains significant business interests in Kunar (gemstones and timber).

Haji Jon Dod: A gemstones and timber smuggler from the Safi tribe, Jon Dod has real estate interests in Jalalabad and Kabul. He is a former border police commander who fought in Panjsher under Massoud and Rabbani. He was governor of Kunar for a short time and is cooperative with the PRT.

"Marble" Jon Dod: Originally from Pech Valley, Safi tribe, Dod bought land in Khas Kunar to run a marble production facility. He was jailed by coalition forces for three years but released. He is very rich.

Criminals/Insurgents

Kashmir Khan: From Shigal district, Shinwari tribe, he was once deputy commander of HIG, and is a consistently loyal commander of Hekmatyar. Considered the most powerful figure in the Asmar Valley, he staunchly opposed the Soviet occupation, the Rabbani government, and the Taliban. People respect him because he did not abuse his power or cut deals with occupiers. He opposes coalition forces.

Haji Matin: Native to the valley and Korengali tribe, Matin is an insurgent leader of the Korengal Valley. He controls export of timber from the valley. His power does not extend beyond the Korengal.

Abu Ikhlas: Iklas is an Arab insurgent leader who came to Kunar to fight the Soviets and grew to prominence with the Salafists. He reportedly married a Kunar girl and has lived in Asadabad for more than 20 years. He coordinates the insurgency with Arab leaders in Kunar.

Table 2. Provincial Government

NAME	POSITION	PHONE #
Fazlullah Wahidi	Provincial Governor	0700-277-766
Noor Mohammad Khan	Deputy Governor	0700-640-660
Gen. Abdul Jalal Jalal	Police Chief	070-212-245
Mawlana Fazlullah	NDS Chief	N/A
Eng. Ameenudeen	RRD Chief	N/A
Farooq Jahan	Economy Director	N/A
Hazrat Khan	Director of Da-Afg Bank	0700-020-668
Haji Sayed Jalal	Chamber of Commerce	N/A
Abdul Ghafoor	Finance Chief	N/A
Marhaba Karimi	Women's Affairs	N/A
Abdullah	Electricity Director	0700-168-366
Haji Dost Mohammad	Border And Tribes Director	N/A
Abdul Qaioum Hakimzi	Culture and Information	070-060-994
Haji Mohammad Ruzi	PTS Chief	N/A
Eng. Mohammad Rahim	Public Works Director	N/A
Haji Sardar Khan	Refugees Director	0700-641-853
Mohammad Anwar	Haj and Mosque	0700-665-746
Haji Muhsil Khan	Agriculture Director	0700-642-400
Rasheedullah Zalmi	Irrigation Director	N/A
Asadullah Fazli	Director Of Public Health	0700-640-881
Mavli Ataullah Noori	Disabilities Director	0700-642-164
Asadullah Roya	Education Director	0700-144-324

The Naktar, a coniferous tree common in Kunar and Nuristan, is popular for construction and making furniture. Illegal logging continues in Kunar, funding insurgents, criminals, and crooked politicians.

PHOTO BY MICHELLE PARKER

Chapter 4
The Economy

Kunar is a traditional agricultural area where the majority of people struggle to feed their large families as subsistence farmers, primarily growing wheat and raising livestock. The basic infrastructure (including water and sanitation, energy, transport, and communications) is inadequate as a basis for private sector expansion.

Economic hardship is a driving factor for decision-making. Basic food supplies like wheat, rice, and oil are imported from Pakistan, and rising prices there are driving some people to desperation. Malnutrition affects at least 38 percent of the population, and up to 25 percent of families report having to borrow money to pay for food.

Arable land is limited and families expand rapidly. Each woman bears an average of nine children. Little economic data exists, but lack of infrastructure and industry clearly lead to unemployment and pervasive criminal activity, particularly smuggling.

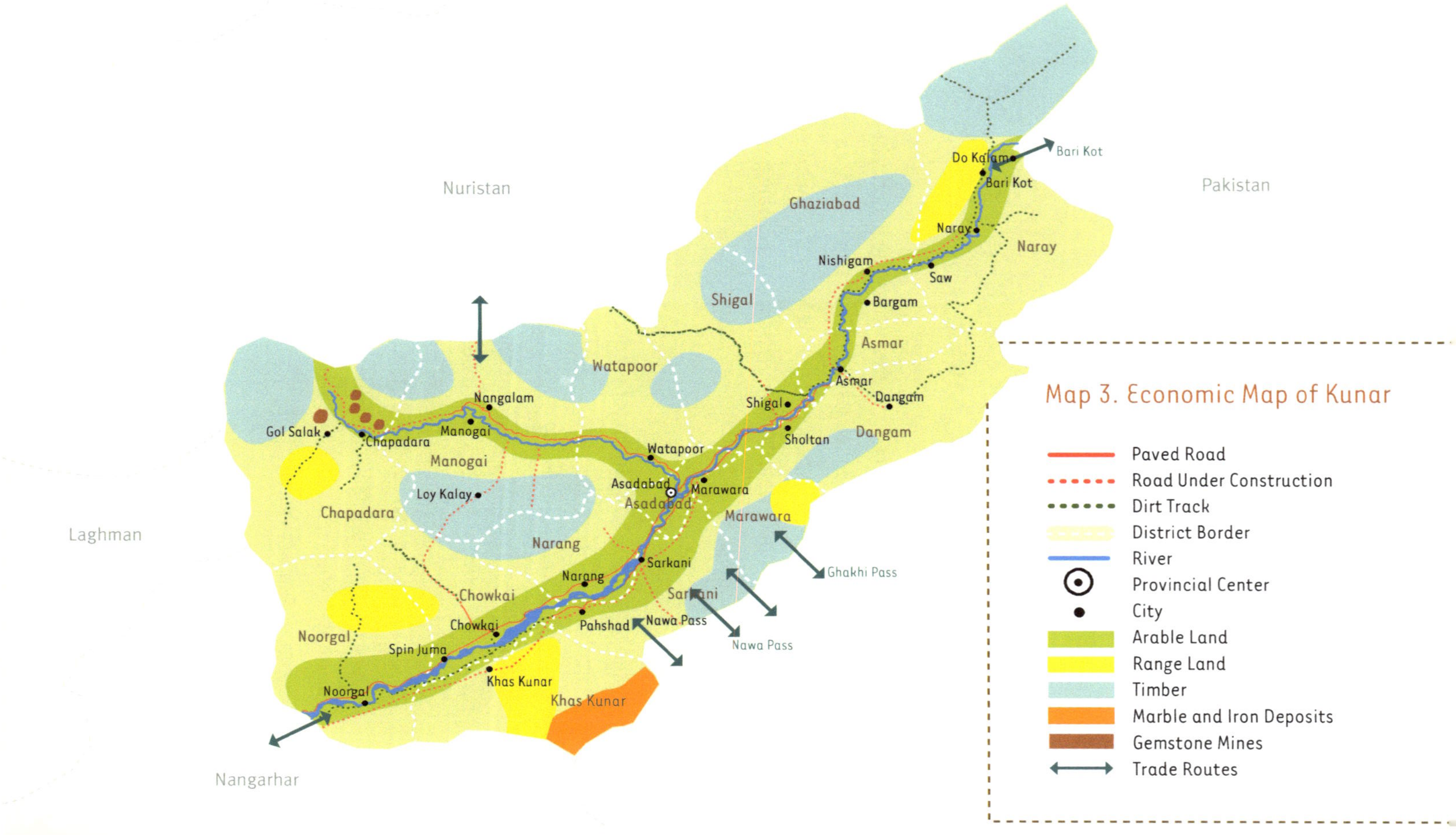

Map 3. Economic Map of Kunar

Legend:
- Paved Road
- Road Under Construction
- Dirt Track
- District Border
- River
- Provincial Center
- City
- Arable Land
- Range Land
- Timber
- Marble and Iron Deposits
- Gemstone Mines
- Trade Routes

Pakistan

Nuristan

Laghman

Nangarhar

Bari Kot

Do Kalam
Bari Kot
Naray
Naray
Saw
Bargam
Nishigam
Asmar
Asmar
Dangam
Dangam
Sholtan
Shigal
Marawara
Marawara
Watapoor
Asadabad
Asadabad
Sarkani
Sarkani
Ghakhi Pass
Nawa Pass
Nawa Pass
Narang
Narang
Pahshad
Khas Kunar
Nangalam
Manogai
Chowkai
Chowkai
Khas Kunar
Loy Kalay
Manogai
Chapadara
Chapadara
Spin Juma
Noorgal
Noorgal
Gol Salak
Watapoor

INFRASTRUCTURE

Energy

A key obstacle to economic development is the lack of electricity. About 41 percent percent of households have access to electricity, mostly through micro-hydro projects at the village level or from diesel generators. No public provision of electricity exists outside of a small part of Asadabad. USAID worked with the PRT and local officials to restore the turbine powering part of Asadabad in late 2008. Plans exist for a major hydroelectric project in the Pech Valley, but funding has been stalled indefinitely. Without energy for productive power, no manufacturing can be done.

Telecommunications

Mobile phones are wildly popular, generally reliable, and cheap. The private companies offering service in Kunar (AWCC, Roshan, and Areeba) are fast expanding, putting up new towers in increasingly remote locations. Internet service is popular but very limited. A few internet cafes cater to young men in Asadabad, Chowkai, Khas Kunar, and Noorgal.

Roads

The PRT has made a profound impact on Kunar with its focused road- and bridge-building campaigns in recent years. Kunar's relatively small land area was dangerous and difficult to traverse due to rugged mountains and rough roads, but now paved roads connect most of the districts in a few hours or less. The five bridges built with US government funds in the past two years are also revolutionizing transport. Officials are pushing for a new border crossing at Nawa Pass to relieve the congestion at Torkham Gate in Nangarhar. This border crossing would be an enormous boost for Kunar's economy.

KEY ECONOMIC SECTORS

Agriculture and Livestock

Kunar has good, fertile soil, but farmers typically use antiquated methods and lack robust seeds, a problem acknowledged by the Director of Agriculture, Irrigation and Livestock. There is no cold storage, and farm-to-market transport is difficult, so most products are consumed or sold locally. Each valley has an elaborate, hand-dug irrigation system, and farmers are working to restore *karez* (underground canal) systems in some districts, such as Marawara.

Large landowners lease small plots to landless people, essentially sharecropping. The main crops are wheat, rice, millet, corn, and beans. Many types of fruits are grown, particularly apples, oranges, grapes, plums, and apricots. Walnuts (Chapadara, Pech Valleys) and almonds (Shuriak Valley) can also be found in certain areas. Most families also raise livestock and some rely exclusively on livestock for their livelihoods. Some tribes, such as the Gujars, are herders. Any excess crops are generally sold in Jalalabad, where prices are a bit higher than in Kunar.

USAID and USDA are both working with Afghan officials and communities to improve agriculture practices.

Timber

Kunar and Nuristan are home to the last extensive forests in Afghanistan. Under Afghan law all forests belong to the government and logging is banned, yet forests are being stripped at an alarming rate with profound environmental implications. A coniferous tree called "nakhtar" in Pashto is valued for use in construction and furniture making and provides a source of funding for insurgent leaders, criminals, and crooked politicians. It is mostly found in the districts of Manogai (including the Korengal Valley), Chapadara, Asmar, Ghaziabad, Naray, and Shigal. Chapadara is perhaps the most heavily forested area, but the people of Chapadara prefer to preserve the forests and do not allow logging. The Shigal people have done the same, though there are fewer forests in Shigal. The provincial government is struggling to come to an accord with the people of the Korengal Valley, who have earned their wealth primarily through timber sales in recent decades and are bitterly opposed to the government's ban on logging.

After agriculture, the largest sector of the economy is the illegal trade of timber and gemstones.

Precious Stones

Emeralds, aquamarine, tourmaline, rubies, and kunzite are found in Kunar, mostly in the Pech River Valley. In theory, their extraction and sale is regulated, but smuggling is rampant. Powerful ex-commanders run their own small empires, operating mines and freely transporting stones to Pakistan. Police and government officials have been known to take part in the trade.

Some of the key players in the gem industry are Matiullah Khan, Haji Gul Dad, and Haji Naqibullah. The centers of activity are Gol Salak in Chapadara and Nangalam in Manogai.

TRENDS AND RELEVANT ISSUES FOR KUNAR TODAY

Timber Management

Governor Wahidi will have to decide whether to crack down on the smuggling trade and face the backlash from powerful warlords, criminals, and involved members of the provincial government, or allow it to continue and thereby undermine the authority of the government. Properly regulated, timber could represent a significant source of revenue for the government, but enforcement will upset the balance of power.

Hydropower Potential

Kunar has no electrical grid beyond Asadabad's weak hydropower dam. With no productive power, no industry can develop. Studies reveal potential for large-scale projects that could power the entire Eastern Region, and several plans have been put forward. The Asian Development Bank has tentatively approved the dam at Manogai on the Pech River, but progress has stalled in the very early stages.

Border Crossings

Numerous passes – at least twelve of them well-established – lead from Kunar into Pakistan. Only three are controlled at present. The main legal passes are at Ghakhi in Marawara district and Nawa in Sarkani district. Both are undeveloped. The third is in the far north at Do Kalam in Naray district. The PRT is constructing a road through the Nawa Pass, which could have an enormous economic impact since Torkham Gate in Nangarhar is severely overcrowded. Nawa Pass could be a viable alternative route between Pakistan and Kabul.

There is no public provision of electricity outside Asadabad, presenting a serious obstacle to economic development. About 40 percent of Kunaris have access to electricity, mostly through micro-hydro power plants or diesel generators.

PHOTO BY MARINA KIELPINSKI

Chapter 5
International Organizations and Reconstruction Activity

PROVINCIAL RECONSTRUCTION TEAM (PRT)

Kunar has an ISAF PRT (US) just south of Asadabad at Camp Wright (locally known as Topchi). The military side consists of a Civil Affairs (CA) team, public affairs team, engineers, and support elements. The civilian component consists of representatives from US Department of State (DoS), US Agency for International Development (USAID), and US Department of Agriculture (USDA). The mission of the PRT is to "assist the Islamic Republic of Afghanistan to extend its authority, in order to facilitate the development of a stable and secure environment in the identified area of operations, and enable Security Sector Reform and reconstruction efforts."

The stated focus of US government efforts in Kunar, which the PRT is tasked to support, is:

Security: ANP training and equipping is done at PRT Asadabad, and US Marines are training the ANA.

Governance: The PRT mentors the provincial authorities wherever possible and works to improve relations between formal government and traditional systems of authority.

Population: The PRT uses information campaigns, assistance programs, and economic opportunities to persuade people to support their government.

Economics: Construction of roads and bridges is a core PRT activity in support of economic growth.

Border: The PRT works with the Afghan government to increase control of the border through Security Sector Reform.

The PRT is currently managing a portfolio of roughly $74 million in projects, nearly all of which is spent on construction of key infrastructure (roads, bridges, clinics, and schools). The PRT is actively engaged in local governance, with an office in the governor's compound. USAID funds technical government capacity-building efforts, and the PRT supports the provincial authorities through joint strategic planning. USDA partners with the Department of Agriculture, Irrigation and Livestock. DoS provides overall policy guidance.

PROJECTS AND ACTIVITIES

The US PRT dominates the reconstruction scene, in large part because constant security threats deter NGOs from operating in Kunar. However, projects are carried out less conspicuously with local supervision through USAID, the National Solidarity Program, and several international NGOs with little or no foreign presence in the province. UNAMA has an office near the PRT and assists with information about all agencies operating in the province. The UN also has World Food Program (WFP), High Commission for Refugees (UNHCR), Fund for Population Activities (UNFPA) and Children's Fund (UNICEF) activities in Kunar. GTZ (German Technical Cooperation) supports government capacity-building and implements projects in selected districts.

The PRT typically works closely with the Afghan government and implements longer-term, employment-intensive projects in key infrastructure areas. Maneuver forces execute quick-impact projects to win access and influence locally.

Electricity

USAID is providing the only large-scale electricity support at present by refurbishing the turbine that supplies power to part of Asadabad. The Japanese planned a survey for a massive dam project on the Pech River, but funding has not been forthcoming. Governor Wahidi is lobbying the ministries in Kabul for support in the hydropower sector; Kunar's rivers have potential to supply power to the entire east of Afghanistan. Any large-scale hydropower project will take years to implement, but the lack of a power source prohibits economic development in the province.

On a much smaller scale, micro-hydro systems providing electricity for a small village are very popular. US forces provide some micro-hydros, particularly in the Pech Valley, and communities themselves construct them through the National Solidarity Program.

Transportation

Kunar's relatively small land area makes it possible to have a profound impact by constructing key roads and bridges. The PRT has done this with the Jalalabad-Asadabad highway, which continues up to the northern tip of Kunar, and with the Pech Valley Road, from Asadabad to Chapadara. Most notably, the PRT constructed five new truck bridges connecting communities on the east side of the Kunar River with the main road, enabling trade and easing access to education and medical care.

Most people feed their families through subsistence farming, often growing wheat. Better irrigation systems are key to agricultural development.

PHOTO BY MARINA KIELPINSKI

USAID also has national road-building programs that include Kunar; these are typically gravel roads and on a smaller scale. The US Army Corps of Engineers also constructs roads, and is currently working on several within Kunar, notably on the east side of the Kunar River connecting Khas Kunar with Marawara, and another leading from Chapadara north to Nuristan province.

The National Solidarity Program supports communities to build village roads and small bridges, including footbridges; the Department of Rural Rehabilitation & Development (DRRD) director maintains updated information on project progress in all areas. GTZ has also constructed bridges in Naray district.

Irrigation

Irrigation is the key priority for the DRRD, and of course for the Department of Agriculture, Irrigation, and Livestock (DAIL). Kunar depends on agriculture for its livelihood, and irrigation systems are crumbling and insufficient. In times of drought the lack of irrigation is devastating. Multiple agencies are working on irrigation at some level: USAID (through the LGCD program), NSP (small community-based projects), and various NGO efforts. USDA recognizes the need to address the irrigation needs as well, and is working on project proposals to reconstruct karez systems and larger canals.

Irrigation has always been the lifeblood of Afghan farmers, and the communities traditionally dedicate certain days to working on the canals and maintaining the system. A "water boss" is designated by the community to manage the system and collect any fees for repairs. Unfortunately that system was broken down during decades of war and chaos. Any attempts to assist with irrigation should begin with community buy-in and a maintenance plan.

Education

There are 295 primary and secondary schools in the province serving 88,701 students (67 percent of students are boys and 76 percent of the schools are boys' schools). Kunar residents consistently display a hunger for education and send their boys and girls to school if there is one within walking distance. However, the government estimates that only 43 percent of children attend school. Just five percent of the 2,572 registered teachers are women, a fact that prevents many conservative families from sending their daughters to school. The overall literacy rates for men and women are 49 percent and 16 percent, respectively.

The Department of Education has a comprehensive list of schools needed in Kunar. The existing buildings are usually overcrowded, and many "schools" are held outdoors or in a mosque.

The PRT has dedicated significant resources to constructing new school buildings, coordinating with the Department of Education for staffing and operation of the schools. The Japanese government also focuses on school-building, and the Indian government made a political statement in 2008 by announcing a plan to construct several schools adjacent to the border with Pakistan.

NGOs also build and equip schools occasionally. The Director of Education coordinates all school-related projects.

Healthcare

The following types of health facilities are provided by the Ministry of Health:

Basic Health Centers (BHCs): Serves a population of up to 30,000 people. Outpatient care only, similar to Level I military care. Basic OB/

GYN, routine immunizations, childhood diseases, treatment of malaria, TB, and care for mental health patients and disabled patients.

Comprehensive Health Clinics (CHCs): Serves a population of up to 60,000 people. Similar to Level II military care. Limited inpatient care, basic laboratory, severe childhood illnesses, malaria. Staffed with male and female doctors, nurses, midwives, lab, and pharmacy techs.

There is no **District/Provincial Level Hospital** in Kunar to provide any higher level of care. The nearest such facility is in Jalalabad.

Healthcare has steadily improved in Kunar with the support of the central government and international donors. Basic health clinics serve people in all 14 districts, and Asadabad has a comprehensive health clinic (often referred to as "the hospital") that serves as a referral center. Still, as of 2007, only 23 percent of the population could access health care within five kilometers of their homes.

The French NGO Aide Medicale Internationale (AMI) partners with the Department of Public Health (DoPH) to implement the national health care plan in Kunar. AMI staffs and manages the clinics in partnership with DoPH. The PRT has prioritized health care, constructing new buildings for the clinics and coordinating closely with DoPH.

NATIONAL SOLIDARITY PROGRAM

The National Solidarity Program (NSP) is run by the Ministry of Rural Rehabilitation & Development (MRRD) and is widely acknowledged as the most successful and effective Afghan-led development program in history. Funded by multiple nations through the World Bank, NSP funnels small grants to democratically elected community development councils (CDCs) to allow them to address their own development needs.

The program operates in all 34 provinces. Detailed information can be found at their website, *www.nspafghanistan.org*. NSP is supported by international NGOs that guide the communities through the process of electing their CDCs and teach them basic accounting and management skills. The program is in its sixth year and has very positive feedback from communities and observers. US forces may come across NSP projects in the most dangerous areas, with villagers quietly working on their own to build a footbridge or a drinking water system. Questions about NSP should be directed to the Director of RRD, who meets weekly with implementing partners and tracks project progress.

OTHER INTERNATIONAL ACTORS AND PROJECTS

The United Nations operates in several sectors in Kunar and oversees implementation of nationwide plans. UNAMA maintains information on all international organization activity and has an office near the PRT south of Asadabad.

Other donors such as the World Bank, Asian Development Bank, Japanese government, and various NGOs may occasionally have activities in Kunar.

Table 3. International Organizations in Kunar

Name	Contact	Phone	Email
Foundation, International Community Assistant (FINCA)	Burhanudin, Supervisor	0700-653-650	burhan_knr@ yahoo.com
Project for Alternative Livelihoods in Eastern Afgh. (GTZ IS PAL)	Liaqat Ali, Provincial Coordinator	0700-653-937	liagaali_liagat@ yahoo.com
Mission d'Aide au Développement des Economies Rurales en Afghanistan (MADERA)	Jawhar Shah"Jalali", Provincial Coordinator	0797-635-482	madera_knpc@ yahoo.com
Relief International (RI)	Ghulam Yahya, Provincial Manager	0700-628-282	ghulam_ yahya3007@ yahoo.com
International Foundation for Hope	N/A	N/A	N/A
Development Alternatives, Inc. (DAI)	N/A	0700-633-866	N/A
United Nations Assistance Mission for Afghanistan (UNAMA)	N/A	N/A	N/A
Food and Agriculture Organization (FAO UN)	N/A	N/A	N/A

A tailor reads Sada-e Azadi, the ISAF newspaper published every two weeks and distributed throughout the province. With low literacy rates, radio remains the most popular news medium. Kunar continues to be an oral culture, where discussions over tea and the Friday sermon are trusted over any radio or television personality.

PHOTO BY MARINA KIELPINSKI

Chapter 6
Information and Influence

MEDIA ACTIVITY AND INFLUENCE

Kunar is a tight-knit and geographically concentrated province, where most information passes by word of mouth. Friday sermons at the mosques remain the most important source of information exchange, as in most of rural Afghanistan. Kunar also has a relatively active media, with local representatives from several international outlets and a core of journalists who report on government activities. Radio is by far the most important medium; nearly everyone has a radio or has access to one, and stations can reach the entire province. Television is limited to Asadabad, and there is no tradition of reading the newspaper.

Little independent journalism exists; most journalists closely follow government activities and refrain from criticism. The concept of investigative journalism has not yet caught on. As a result, journalists are respected but viewed as a part of the government.

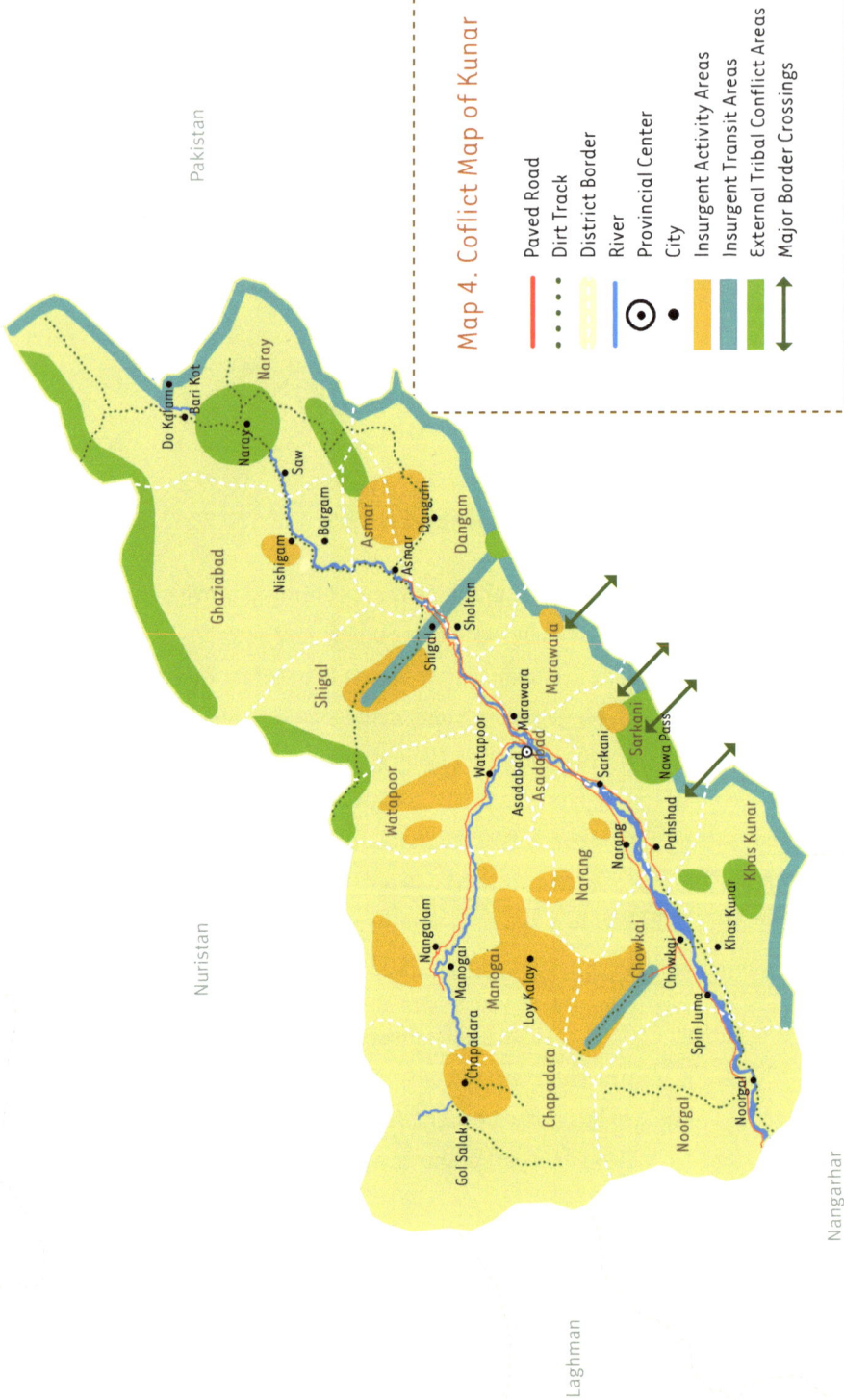

Map 4. Coflict Map of Kunar

Paved Road
Dirt Track
District Border
River
Provincial Center
City
Insurgent Activity Areas
Insurgent Transit Areas
External Tribal Conflict Areas
Major Border Crossings

Pakistan

Nuristan

Laghman

Nangarhar

Do Kalam
Bari Kot
Naray
Naray
Saw
Burgam
Nishigam
Asmar
Dangam
Asmar
Dangam
Ghaziabad
Sholtan
Shigal
Shigal
Marawara
Watapoor
Marawara
Asadabad
Asadabad
Sarkani
Sarkani
Nawa Pass
Watapoor
Narang
Pahshad
Khas Kunar
Nangalam
Narang
Manogai
Chowkai
Khas Kunar
Manogai
Chowkai
Loy Kalay
Chapadara
Chowkai
Spin Juma
Gol Salak
Chapadara
Noorgal
Noorgal
Noorgal

Local journalists work together regularly and share information. Many of them take part in writers' and poets' societies in their spare time. There are several active journalists' associations in Kunar, but they are weak.

Newspapers and magazines are printed in Jalalabad or Kabul. The PRT bought a printing press for the Department of Information and Culture, but it is still unused at the time of writing due to a lack of operational knowledge.

Radio

At least six radio stations broadcast in Kunar. Kunar Radio, part of RTA (Radio and Television Afghanistan), is the government station. It is on 12 hours each day (AM/FM) and reaches all the districts. It is very popular, with a variety of news, religious programming, and poetry in the weekly schedule. People get international news from the BBC and Voice of America, which both broadcast 24 hours a day. Voice of Liberty and Arman FM are also popular but do not reach the districts. Zala FM has recently begun broadcasting from Asadabad.

Television

Television is mostly restricted to Asadabad since people in the districts typically cannot afford a satellite dish and do not have electricity. The Kabul-based Tolo TV is very popular and can be viewed without a satellite dish.

Newspaper

There is no tradition of reading the newspaper in Kunar, but people are generally eager to see anything in print. Sada-e Azadi, the ISAF newspaper, is published every two weeks and distributed province-wide. A few people in Asadabad read Pakistani newspapers that can be bought in Jalalabad. The provincial government produces a somewhat irregular weekly newsletter in Asadabad for distribution among government officials.

INFORMATION SHARING NETWORKS

Kunar's dense population and tribal networks mean that information travels quickly, and everyone usually knows what everyone else is doing, from Pakistan's tribal agencies to the farthest reaches of Kunar. Most people get their information via word of mouth, through friends and family, village leaders, and on Fridays at the mosque.

Kunar is still largely an oral culture (most people are illiterate), so the custom is to sit and discuss current events, usually over a cup of tea. Afghans enjoy discussing issues among themselves, and foreigners often make the mistake of rushing conversations in the effort to gain information. The real substance of a discussion will not come out for some time, and only after securing trust. Rumors surface quickly and are often repeated. Kunaris will often tell foreigners what they imagine they want to hear, whether through politeness or expediency.

As widespread as radio and television have become, it is doubtful that they equal the influence of the mullahs and their Friday sermons, which penetrate every week into even the most remote villages. More importantly, no radio or television personality has the moral authority and trust of the population that the local mullah has. It is important to be aware of what is being said in mosques to ensure that religious leaders understand the goals of the international community in Afghanistan and to ensure that Islam is respected at all times.

The lack of electricity limits television's influence, but the radio is widely heard in every district. People are hungry for information, and journalists are generally respected and free to travel and do their work. Coalition forces and insurgents both use information campaigns to win influence over contested areas. The US bases at Nangalam and Naray have their own radio stations. The Taliban also conducts information warfare by distributing night letters and leaflets. Taliban leaders often telephone local journalists to report their activities. Occasionally the Taliban threatens journalists, but none have been harmed yet.

The Afghan National Police (ANP) is undermanned and ill-equipped, hampered by corruption, absence of accountability, and inadequate pay. While US forces are training and equipping the ANP, many police do not yet command the respect of the people.

PHOTO BY STAFF SGT. JOSHUA T JASPER

Chapter 7
Big Issues

ECONOMIC UNDERDEVELOPMENT

The insurgency in Kunar is rooted more in economics than ideology. Unemployment is widespread, and there are few legal economic opportunities. Desperately poor young men are easily recruited to conduct attacks for insurgents. Poverty is at the root of systemic social problems, such as poor nutrition and health care, failure to pursue education, and forced marriages.

Kunar also has finite land resources and a fast-expanding population. People fight over limited resources, particularly water and agricultural land. The vast majority of families are still struggling to feed their families as subsistence farmers. New economic opportunities must be created to sustain the existing population in Kunar.

Development projects in Kunar are changing the face of the province, particularly by connecting the communities on the east side of the Kunar River with the rest of the province (and the country). Kunar is a natural transportation route between Pakistan's tribal areas and Afghanistan, offering an alternative to Torkham Gate. But development of transport and trade at any significant level depends upon stability on the Pakistan side of the border – an unlikely prospect in the short term.

Kunar needs investment in its infrastructure – both human and physical – to induce economic development. Roads and bridges are easing movement and encouraging commerce. Kunar also needs to produce something more than subsistence farming. A reliable source of power will be key to setting the province on its own economic footing. Efforts to improve education for Kunar's people at all levels and move beyond subsistence living will be extremely important in the long term.

NASCENT SECURITY FORCES

The continued weakness of the ANP remains a significant impediment to progress. Until the ANA raises a larger force, the ANP will be on the front lines of the counterinsurgency fight, undermanned and ill-equipped. The force is made up primarily of individuals seeking economic opportunity, with some exceptions among the senior-level officers. Opportunities for corruption, an absence of accountability, and inadequate pay have a corrosive effect on performance. The force is further hindered by the lack of a functioning judicial and corrections system, competition from other armed groups, and inadequate government support.

US efforts to mentor and equip the ANSF and its shift in focus to supporting the ABP are increasing with the rise in troops. Increased ANA and ABP presence along the border is likely to help stabilize Kunar as insurgent transit routes are blocked. These investments in training and equipping are already bearing fruit; ANSF are able to conduct more operations independently, and the ANA has secured a professional reputation among the people. But support to ANSF will have to continue intensively for years to come.

TIMBER AND GEMSTONES SMUGGLING

Timber is by far the most important commodity smuggled. A few powerful men run the lucrative timber trade. It is illegal, but no government oversight or enforcement regime has been able to control it successfully. Attempts to legally auction off the existing timber in Kunar's lumberyards have not met much success. The trade fuels the decimation of a key natural resource, finances criminal activity and insurgency, and undermines the government's authority – particularly because the public believes that the government itself condones and profits from timber smuggling.

The fact that gemstones and timber are mostly smuggled to Pakistan outside of government purview robs the government of a potentially valuable tax base. A total ban on timber harvesting would harm the carpentry industry, one of Kunar's only employment sectors. The Korengali people continue to resist both GIRoA and US forces as long as they are prevented from selling timber, as it is their only source of wealth. But without clear, enforceable laws, the timber trade will continue to be detrimental to Kunar's development. Ultimately, the timber issue is a government question. GIRoA will have to decide whether to enforce or change the existing laws.

WEAK GOVERNANCE

Provincial and district government officials have limited or no capacity or resources for delivering services or responding to their constituents. Economic vulnerability and a lack of transparent financial, legal, and administrative systems create incentives for corruption. Motivated by a desire for money, access to power and influence, and ensuring job security, government officials at all levels are likely to seek financial gain instead of serving the public. With access to funding sources, constant

Kunar's infrastructure is currently inadequate as a basis for development. Road, irrigation, and power projects are three of the top priorities.

PHOTO BY CAPT GERALDO GONZALEZ

donor staff turnover, and consistent absence of penalties for corrupt behavior, officials find it possible to enrich themselves and others or to work for the benefit of one group over others. Lack of confidence in the government enables the insurgents to gain support.

Many government officials are essentially untrained and are not capable of executing the key elements of their jobs (administration, budgeting, planning, implementation, etc.). Targeted programs focus on capacity building for these officials, but it will take time. Aid programs are beginning to demand more from government officials while holding them accountable; any US-funded interventions should support this approach.

POROUS BORDER

The border is a very fluid concept in Kunar, and nearly every issue that affects the province is related to its situation on the border. Timber and gemstone smuggling, insurgent traffic, poppy and weapons smuggling, and licit commerce all depend on unimpeded border crossings. Tribal, familial, and political ties mean events on the other side of the border can have an impact on Kunar as well. Permanent ANA battalions on the east side of the river, plus the five new bridges that will be completed in 2009, could fundamentally change the dynamics of the border and the districts along it.

Bridges will increase commerce and enable ANSF to regularly patrol the volatile east side of the river. But instability in Pakistan, particularly in the Bajaur Agency, allows insurgents a safe haven for conducting attacks in Afghanistan.

During the spring and summer months, men spend their days working in the fields and tending livestock. Daily life slows after the harvest, with men spending most of their time hanging around with friends or at the mosque.

PHOTO BY MARINA KIELPINSKI

Appendices

COMMON COMPLIMENTS REGARDING THE US MILITARY IN THE EASTERN REGION

- Afghans respect the US forces for leaving their families to come and help them.

- Afghans compliment the US forces' work ethic and say it drives them to work harder for themselves.

- Afghans appreciate projects such as roads that change their lives for the better after decades of war.

- Other foreign armies have come to conquer; the US military has come to help Afghans.

COMMON COMPLAINTS REGARDING THE US MILITARY IN THE EASTERN REGION

- Afghans claim that when the Americans are attacked by insurgents, they sometimes retaliate against innocent people.

- Afghans claim that the coalition has inflicted excessive civilian casualties while taking out few insurgent leaders.

- Afghans complain that the US forces raid their houses at night without cause or government support.

- Afghans believe Americans use informers for their intelligence gathering who are not being honest. Most of these people have their own agendas and manipulate the truth.

- Afghans lament that coalition forces and other foreign personnel do not know or understand the local people and what is going on among them.

- Afghans complain that US forces drive them off the roads and drive too carelessly.

TIMELINE OF KEY EVENTS

October 2001: Taliban flee Kunar; Haji Jon Dod claims governor's office.

April 2002: Yusuf Shah Juhan appointed governor of Kunar by new Karzai government.

February 2004: US PRT set up at Camp Wright, just south of Asadabad.

June 2005: US Navy SEALS ambushed in Shuriak Valley in worst disaster in SEAL history.

Late 2005: Asadullah Wafa appointed governor.

April 2006: 10th Mountain Division sets up first battalion-sized elements in Kunar at Camp Blessing and Naray.

September 2006: Shalizai Deedar appointed governor.

November 2007: Sayed Fazlullah Wahidi appointed governor, representing a notable shift to modern methods of governance.

February 2008: Three ANA kandaks permanently assigned to Kunar province.

February 2008: PRT opens offices in the governor's compound in downtown Asadabad.

March 2008: Kunar Construction Center, a US government project, graduates its first class in Shigal.

May – June 2008: Pakistani government goes on offensive against Taliban militants in FATA and NWFP; an estimated 50,000 refugees cross into Kunar to flee the fighting.

July 2008: US outpost at Want in the Waygal Valley attacked; nine US soldiers killed as it is nearly overrun.

May 2009: Militants launch coordinated attack on US outpost in Ghaziabad district, killing three US troops, two Latvians, and four Afghan soldiers and an interpreter.

DAY IN THE LIFE OF A RURAL KUNARI

The typical rural household in Kunar wakes up before dawn for the first prayers of the day. Men wash and go to the mosque for prayers, while women build a fire, take care of the children, and pray at home. Breakfast is usually bread and green tea. Families with animals may have eggs or milk as well.

After breakfast, men go to work, usually in the fields. Women prepare the children for school if they are fortunate enough to have a school nearby. Boys are much more likely to go to school than girls. Girls often stay at home and do household work with their siblings during the day. Boys not attending school are sent to run errands or to work with their father in the fields. Young children of either sex are responsible for tending cattle, sheep, and goats.

Women typically only leave the home compound for special occasions (weddings or festivals), though in a few parts of rural Kunar women do field work at certain times of the year. Women pray five times a day, inside the home. On Fridays they may visit the homes of close relatives, praying together and chatting over tea. The rest of their time is spent in taking care of children, preparing food, and cleaning the compound.

Men are in charge of the livestock, or some work outside of the home as shopkeepers, teachers, or manual laborers. Men typically have lunch with other men, discussing events of the day, or return home for a quick lunch before returning to work. There is usually time for a short nap in the afternoon, particularly in the heat of the summer. At dusk the men return home for dinner, which usually consists of more bread with *palau* (boiled rice with a bit of meat). In the spring and summer vegetables are also eaten. Families eat the evening meal together and, after washing, settle in to sleep on mats on the floor, typically in a common room.

In winter months, after harvesting and settling in, daily life slows. Women tend to household chores; men hang out around the mosque or with friends.

FURTHER READING AND SOURCES

Books

- *ISAF PRT Handbook*, 3rd Ed. February 2007. NATO.

- Louis Dupree, *Afghanistan,* Princeton: Princeton University Press, 1979.

- Edward Girardet and Jonathan Walter, *Afghanistan: Essential Field Guides to Humanitarian and conflict zones*, CROSSLINES Publication Ltd., 1998 and 2004, *www.crosslinesguides.com*.

- Ahmed Rashid, *Taliban: Militant Islam, Oil and Fundamentalism in Central Asia*, 2001.

- Ahmed Rashid, *Descent into Chaos: The United States and the Future of Nation Building in Afghanistan, Pakistan, and Central Asia*, Viking Press, 2008.

- Larry Goodson, *Afghistan's Endless War: State Failure, Regional Politics, and the Rise of the Taliban*, 2001.

- Greg Mortenson, *Three Cups of Tea: One Man's Mission to Promote Peace ...One School at a Time*, 2007.

- Barnett Rubin, 1) *The Fragmentation of Afghanistan* and 2) *Afghanistan's Uncertain Transition from Turmoil to Normalcy*, 2001 and 2007.

- Michael Griffin, *Reaping the Whirlwind: The Taliban Movement in Afghanistan*, London: Pluto Press, 2001.

- Steve Coll, *Ghost Wars: The Secret History of the CIA, Afghanistan, and Bin Laden, From the Soviet Invasion to September 10, 2001*, New York Penquin Press, 2004.

- Ben Macintyre, *The Man Who Would Be King: The First American in Afghanistan*, New York: Farrar, Straus and Giroux, 2005.

Articles

- Asger Christensen. The Pashtuns of Kunar: Tribe, Class, and Community Organization, Afghanistan Journal, Vol 7, No. 3, 1980.

- The Afghanistan National Development Strategy, President Karzai, 2006, *www.reliefweb.int/rw/RWFiles2006.nsf/ FilesByRWDocUNIDFileName/KHII-6LK3R2-unama-afg-30jan2. pdf/$File/unama-afg-30jan2.pdf*

- Elections in 2009 and 2010: Technical and Contextual Challenges to Building Democracy in Afghanistan Afghanistan Research and Evaluation Unit, November 2008 *www.areu.org.af/index.php?option=com_docman&Itemid=26&task=doc_download&gid=612* -

- Potential Analysis of the Eastern Region and Nangarhar Province and Implication in Programming, Raphy Favre. *www.aizon.org/Nangarhar%20Potential%20Analysis.pdf*

- *Mines and Mineral Occurrences of Afghanistan,* compiled by G.H. Orris and J.D. Bliss, open-file report 02-110, US Geological Survey, US Department of the Interior, 2002.

Web Sites

- Afghanistan Research and Evaluation Unit (publishes the Afghanistan A to Z guide) *www.areu.org.af/index.php?option=com_frontpage&Itemid=25*

- Afghanistan Information Management Services *www.aims.org.af*

- Afghanstan Online (Links to Official GIRoA and embassy websites) *www.afghan-web.com/politics*

- Naval Postgraduate School Program for Culture and Conflict Studies *www.nps.edu/Programs/CCS/index.html*

- USAID *www.usaid.gov/locations/asia/countries/afghanistan*

- Richard Strand's Nuristan, Hidden Land of the Hindu Kush *http://users.sedona.net/~strand*

- National Solidarity Program *www.nspafghanistan.org*

www.ingramcontent.com/pod-product-compliance
Lightning Source LLC
Chambersburg PA
CBHW040128270326
41927CB00001B/27